ANCIENT SENTINELS

THE SEQUOIAS OF
YOSEMITE NATIONAL PARK

by H. THOMAS HARVEY

Revised and Updated
by BILL KUHN and
PETE DEVINE

Yosemite Conservancy
YOSEMITE NATIONAL PARK

YOSEMITE
CONSERVANCY.

yosemiteconservancy.org

Yosemite Conservancy inspires people to support projects and programs that
preserve Yosemite and enrich the visitor experience.

Cover design by Eric Ball Design

Interior design by Nancy Austin Design

Maps courtesy of Leslie Stone Associates

ISBN 978-1-930238-64-0

Manufactured using recycled papers

Printed in China by Toppan Leefung

1 2 3 4 5 6 – 22 21 20 19 18

MIX
Paper from
responsible sources
FSC® C104723

CONTENTS

THE GIANT SEQUOIA

Discovery

GIANT SEQUOIAS were first encountered long before Europeans colonized the Americas. Generation after generation, people in the Sierra Nevada lived with these big trees. The first giant sequoias seen by European Americans were those in Calaveras County, north of Yosemite. In 1833, an exploratory party led by mountain man Joseph Walker likely passed through the North Calaveras Grove; it is even possible that explorer Jed Smith had seen these same trees in 1827. For many years it was believed that the Walker Party came through the Yosemite region and encountered the Merced and/or Tuolumne Groves, but more scholarship has suggested an alternative route of their Sierra Nevada transit well to the north. A clerk on the trip, Zenas Leonard, wrote in his journal, "In the last two days travelling we have found some trees of the Red-wood species, incredibly large—some of which would measure from 16 to 18 fathoms [96 to 108 feet or 29.5 to 33 m] round the trunk at the height of a man's head from the ground." Leonard's journal was published in 1839, but copies were scarce and did not receive much attention until 1904, by which time other, more publicized encounters with giant sequoias had been had. None of the Walker party was especially literate or interested in publicity, and none of them impressed others with their unique find.[1]

The North Calaveras Grove was again entered by two other groups in 1850, but this news didn't reach the world beyond the frenzy of the Gold Rush. This left the way open for Augustus T. Dowd to go down in history books. In 1852 he came upon the North Calaveras Grove of giant sequoias in the Mother Lode Country (now protected in Calaveras Big Trees State Park). As the story goes, he was unable

The Grizzly Giant, Mariposa Grove.
Photo: © Stephen Dacosta

Galen Clark with one of the trees he loved. *Photo credit can be found on page 2.*

to convince his fellow employees at the Union Water Company in Murphys of his magnificent find. So Dowd made up a story about having shot a huge grizzly bear and said he needed help to bring in the meat. This lured the unsuspecting confirmers to the site of the big trees. An article in the *Sonora Herald* in June of 1852 then proclaimed the discovery to California. This established what is generally accepted as the "effective discovery date," given that Leonard's earlier account went unread or unheeded. Dowd's find was soon known around the world.

Then a curious thing happened. Numerous early explorers stepped forward to claim they had seen the trees at an earlier date. Tales of these earlier encounters all had one thing in common: they were written or told after 1852. No record has come to light revealing the thoughts of the Walker party, whose members seemingly had a legitimate claim that they were the first European Americans to have seen these giant trees.

The American Indians, of course, have lived with the giant sequoias for centuries. One name that some of the several Indian groups that lived with sequoias may have used for these trees is *wawona*—perhaps an imitation of the hoot of a great horned owl, the guardian spirit of the giant sequoias. The most famous application of the name *wawona* is to a tunneled tree in the Mariposa Grove, now fallen. A large opening was cut through the base of the live and perfectly healthy Wawona Tree's trunk in 1881, creating a short tunnel through which automobiles once drove. Unfortunately, partly because of the damage done by entrepreneurs, this tree fell in 1969.

The Mariposa Grove appears to have been discovered by European Americans around 1850. Major Burney, the first sheriff of Mariposa County, has been credited with the find, but once again, public recognition shifted through history to another who later publicized the grove. Regardless, it was only the second sequoia grove broadly known to European Americans. In 1857, Galen Clark brought attention to the Mariposa Grove and named it after the county in which it lies. It is generally accepted that he first entered the grove from the northeast and encountered the magnificent specimen that bears his name to this day (see page 37).

In 1856, Clark established a homestead that became a simple hotel in the meadowlands at what later came to be called Wawona and served as a guide for visitors to the Mariposa Grove and Yosemite Valley. He built a cabin in the grove in 1864, and a third-generation replica of that cabin now stands in the same area. Clark, born in 1814, came to California in 1853 to search for gold. He became seriously ill in 1855 and decided to move to the mountains to spend his final days. He recovered, however, and on and off until the age of eighty-three he served as Guardian to the federally established Yosemite Grant (Yosemite Valley and the Mariposa Grove). When he died, just shy of ninety-six, he was buried in the Yosemite Cemetery in Yosemite Valley beneath four giant sequoias he had planted from seedlings years earlier. Now more than 130 years old, these juvenile trees are 24 to 39 inches (60 to 100 cm) in diameter at breast height (a standard often used in measuring the size of tree trunks).

Description of the Giant Sequoia

The giant sequoia begins life as an embryo in a tiny seed. The seed is so tiny in comparison to the mature tree that the ratio in size of the embryo to the mature sequoia is the same as that of the mature tree to the Earth. It takes more than 91,000 such seeds to weigh 1 pound (200,620 seeds per kilogram). The seed itself is made up mostly of nonliving tissue that forms wing-like structures around the central embryo. These wings facilitate long-distance dispersal in the wind. If a seed lands in a favorable location (especially a recently burned location), it may then germinate to

Sequoia cone (typically 1.5 to 2.5 inches or 3.8 to 6.4 cm in length) with seeds, which are similar in size to oatmeal flakes. *Photo: © Yosemite Conservancy/Pete Devine*

produce a diminutive seedling only 1 inch (2.5 cm) high.

Most seedlings have four short, linear seed leaves, similar to short pine needles, though the number may vary from three to six. Within a few weeks, the seedling adds secondary leaves. These juvenile leaves are also linear and rather soft, in contrast to the adult leaves, which

Top: Sequoia seedling. *Photo: © Yosemite Conservancy/Pete Devine*
Bottom: Juvenile sequoias, Mariposa Grove. *Photo: © Yosemite Conservancy/Ryan Kelly*

are wider and circular or elliptic in cross section, stiff, about 0.4 to 0.6 inches (1 to 1.5 cm) long, and sharply pointed. At this early stage, most of the growth is concentrated in the roots rather than the shoots, for those seedlings whose roots reach adequate soil moisture have the best chance of surviving the dry summers and autumns of the Sierra Nevada.

It has been known for generations that, as with most conifers, giant sequoias have broad but shallow root systems. Roots are critical for anchoring such tall, heavy trees, and roots also have to supply small amounts of soil minerals and vast amounts of water to the canopy foliage. Sequoia roots can reach more than 100 feet (30 m) laterally from the tree's trunk, but the great bulk of these extensive underground arms are within 8 feet (2.5 m) of the surface.

Recent research has suggested that sequoias have deeper roots than has heretofore been understood. The Sierra Nevada's dry summers signify that these big trees need to draw water from somewhere other than upper layers of soil that have been soaked with the prior winter's snowmelt; it is unlikely that the known shallow root systems can account for the tremendous water needs of these trees. (Imagine the difficulty, however, of attempting to trace small roots deep beneath such an immense structure.) More study is needed in order to understand the nature of any deeper roots.

As the years pass, seedlings grow into young trees with a graceful, narrow conical form. Often called spire-tops, these striking youngsters have a distinct, full, sharply pointed top. This outline results from rapid upward growth that exceeds lateral, spreading growth. This growth habit is known as excurrent, whereas growth in which all of the terminal shoots grow at the same rate is known as decurrent. An oak tree, with its rounded profile, is a good example of the latter type. Rapid vertical growth is the strategy giant sequoias use to access ample sunshine. This is crucial for survival, as giant sequoias are shade intolerant and will die if they live too long in the shadows of other trees. This stage of growth continues until trees are about one hundred years old. During this time they may bear cones with viable seeds, with a few capable of reproducing at the tender age of ten or fifteen years.

Centuries roll by, and a giant sequoia approaches its maximum height and starts to develop a rounded, dome-like crown. This, too, is a distinctive phase in the giant sequoia's life, and such mature trees can be recognized on the skyline from miles away. Generally, these trees are still in the prime of life.

Among the oldest trees, some can be recognized by a partially dead snag-top. Veterans that have experienced direct lightning strikes to their spire or fires reaching up into their crown characteristically exhibit one or more dead leaders or branches at the top of the tree. Lightning generally fractures the upper crown, while fire is often gentler in its denuding. Root damage usually affects the uppermost water supply and can cause death at the apex. Despite such experiences, many old trees persist with several dead leaders,

Top: The rounded crown of a mature sequoia. Photo: © Yosemite Conservancy/Josh Helling
Bottom: Fire scar. Photo: Courtesy of NPS

offering mute testimony to the tribulations they have survived.

Fire scars are typically most extensively developed on the upslope side of the base of giant sequoias. This is due to the natural accumulation of fuel on that side. In addition, when trees fall on a hillslope, they may roll down and come to rest against the trunks of other sequoias. When fire ignites the fuel, it can then burn hot enough and long enough at the base of the standing trees to consume the bark and kill the living layer beneath. Subsequent fires may enlarge the scar until it consumes the interior of the base of a tree, leaving only bark and the living cambium (which produces the xylem and phloem that transport water and nutrients within the tree). Some trees can have their trunks entirely blackened by fire, but as long as the fire doesn't burn through all of the cambium around the whole circumference, the crown above will continue to live and to grow. Over time, a healthy tree can completely heal over a fire scar.

Even after death, the giant sequoia looms as an imposing figure in the forest. Magnificent stumps or snags are found in most groves. Fallen trees are also impressive and aid in understanding the almost incomprehensible size that the giant sequoia attains. The fallen Wawona Tree and the Fallen Monarch in the Mariposa Grove are examples of grand proportions. Walk alongside one of these fallen giants, and their greatness, both in height and girth, is more fully understood. Their persistence after death is also impressive. Based on its growth rings, one tree was determined to have stood for two thousand years, its dead stump solid and undecayed. Such persistence may have been one thing that enticed John Muir to search (unsuccessfully) for groves now dead that once existed between the present groves.

Size of the Giant Sequoia

The giant sequoia has the distinction of being the largest tree on Earth, past or present, in terms of total volume. The largest known living individual is the General Sherman Tree in Sequoia National Park. It is 275 feet (84 m) tall and has a circumference at ground level of 103 feet (31 m), a diameter at breast height of 25 feet (7.6 m), and a total volume estimated at 52,508 cubic feet (1,487 m^3).

Through a combination of rapid growth and longevity, the giant sequoia reaches its full height at around eight hundred years. If it lives significantly longer, its subsequent growth is mostly in girth, though it may also grow slightly

taller. In other words, the tree adds more bulk than height in its later years. The Grizzly Giant in the Mariposa Grove, for example, is about 31 feet (9.5 m) in diameter at the ground, almost 17 feet (5.2 m) in diameter at 60 feet (18 m) high and more than 13 feet (4 m) at 120 feet (36.5 m) above the base. The General Sherman Tree is more than 12 feet (3.7 m) in diameter 200 feet (61 m) above the base. Thus, the older giant sequoia trees appear as columns—parallel structures supporting the green canopy above them.

Although its close relative the coast redwood is sometimes more than 50 feet (15 m) taller, the giant sequoia still reaches impressive heights. The maximum height for giant sequoias is over 300 feet (91.5 m). The majority of the tallest and oldest giant sequoias in California are more than about 230 feet (70 m) tall. The tallest giant sequoia is believed to be an unnamed tree in the Redwood Mountain Grove of Kings Canyon National Park, standing at 312 feet (95 m) tall. Some of the other tallest giant sequoias include an unnamed tree in the Mariposa Grove at 303 feet (92 m) tall; an unnamed tree in the Merced Grove at just over 299 feet (91 m) tall; and the Diamond Tree, at 286 feet (87 m) tall in the Atwell Grove (Sequoia National Park).

The five largest trees by trunk volume are the General Sherman Tree, at 52,508 cubic feet (1,487 m³), in Sequoia National Park; the General Grant Tree, at 46,608 cubic feet (1,320 m³) in Kings Canyon National Park; the President Tree, at 45,148 cubic feet (1,278 m³) in Sequoia National Park; the Lincoln Tree, at 44,471 cubic feet (1,259 m³) in Sequoia National Park; and the Stagg Tree at 42,557 cubic feet (1,205 m³) in the Alder Creek Grove.[1, 2]

The diameter of a giant sequoia can vary greatly along the base of the tree depending on where it is measured. Due to the unusually large spread of the tree's base, known as butt swell, reported values for diameters close to the ground may vary. In addition, if diameter is measured at ground level, it will be greater for a tree on a slope than it would be if that same tree were on level ground because, on a slope, the plane along which the diameter is measured is slanted, not level. Therefore, diameters taken perpendicular

"Butt swell" of a mature sequoia, Mariposa Grove. *Photo:* © *Yosemite Conservancy/Josh Helling*

to the axis of the tree are preferred for comparative purposes.

Diameters for forest trees are usually taken at 4.5 feet (1.4 m) above the ground on the uphill side. This height is designated the diameter at breast height, or DBH. However, among large specimens of giant sequoia, 4.5 feet (1.4 m) is still usually in the area of the butt swell. Therefore, two alternative methods have been developed for measuring the diameter. One involves selecting an arbitrary height, such as 10 feet (3 m), which is generally above the butt swell. The other involves simply taking diameter measurements above the butt swell, however far up the trunk that might be. The point of all this is that when a diameter is given, the height above the ground must be known in order to interpret the measurement.

The maximum diameter reported for a giant sequoia is 69 feet (21 m) at ground level for the Waterfall Tree in the Alder Creek Grove within Giant Sequoia National Monument. The huge buttress at the bottom of this tree makes it a

true standout. Most of the largest giant sequoias attain a ground-level diameter of 26 to 36 feet (7.9 to 11 m). This includes trees in Yosemite such as the Grizzly Giant, which measures 30.7 feet (9.4) in diameter at ground level. When measurements are taken 20 feet (6.1 m) above the base, and thus well above the butt swell, maximum diameters are about 20 feet (6.1 m). For the largest trees, diameters taken at 4.5 feet (1.4 m) above the base generally range from 25 to 30 feet (7.6 to 9.1 m).

Even the branches of some giant sequoias are remarkable for their size. The Grizzly Giant's largest branch is 6 feet (1.8 m) in diameter, while the General Sherman Tree has a branch 6.8 feet (2.1 m) in diameter and 150 feet (46 m) in length. These branches are larger than the largest specimens of many tree species east of the Mississippi, yet they are inconspicuous parts of these enormous trees.

It's possible to gain a vague impression of the giant sequoia's size from these kinds of statistics. Truly understanding their dimensions, however, is difficult. Perhaps the easiest way to comprehend a tree that is 300 feet (91.5 m) tall and 30 feet (9.1 m) across at its base is to mentally remove the tree from the forest and put it in other surroundings. Imagine for a moment that you are watching a football game. Our imaginary tree, lying on its side, would cover the field from goal line to goal line. Some of its branches would reach into the seats one-third of the way up the stadium. Now let's move the tree (without its prodigious roots) to San Francisco but keep it in its normal, upright position. Standing next to San

TREE SIZE CLASS DEFINITIONS

Adults: greater than 6.5 feet or 79 inches (200 cm) DBH*; generally greater than 200 feet (61 m) tall

Young adults: 39–79 inches (100–200 cm) DBH; generally 100–200 feet (30–61 m) tall

Juveniles: 8–39 inches (20–100 cm) DBH; generally 30–100 feet (9–30 m) tall

Saplings: 1–8 inches (2.5–20 cm) DBH; generally 4–30 feet (1.2–9.1 m) tall

Seedlings: less than 1 inch (2.5 cm) DBH; generally less than 4 feet (1.2 m) tall

*DBH stands for "diameter at breast height," standardized to a height of 4.5 feet (1.4 m).

Francisco City Hall, the top of the tree would be at the same height as the top of the spire atop the hall's dome. If the tree were placed in front of Lower Yosemite Fall, the tops of the tree and fall would be just about even. Or imagine the upright tree in a typical residential neighborhood. From the front porch of a house, the tree would completely block the street, and you wouldn't be able to see the house across the street. If we mentally cut a cross section out of the tree's trunk and set it on its side, it would still be 10 feet (3 m) higher than the top of a two-story house. Now we can put the tree back in the forest with an enlightened appreciation of its awesome size.

Age of the Giant Sequoia

A reasonably close estimate of a tree's age can be obtained by counting its growth rings, which are formed within woody tree stems in areas that have cold winters. The giant sequoia is like the majority of trees in having three distinct layers of tissue in its trunk: the outer bark, the growing and dividing cambium layer just beneath the bark, and the wood that forms the major portion of the mature tree. The cambium is a layer only a few cells thick, measuring less than 0.03 inch (0.8 mm) across. Here, cell division produces phloem (and bark) tissues on the side of the cambium toward the exterior of the tree, and xylem (and wood) tissues toward the interior. The phloem and xylem transport water and nutrients throughout the tree.

Distinct rings arise as growth rates vary with the seasons. As day length increases and temperatures warm in springtime, cell division in the cambium layer begins to accelerate. The new wood cells it produces, called sapwood, toward the center of the tree, are relatively large, with thin, light-colored cell walls. This early wood, as it is called, is less dense. As summer progresses in our Mediterranean climate, and the amount of water available diminishes, the size of newly produced wood cells decreases, and their walls are relatively thick and dark brown in color. This is known as late wood. New cell production ceases when the growing season ends. The result is two bands of cells that constitute an annual ring. The rings are generally easy to distinguish from one another because the light, porous early wood produced by rapid growth in spring

An interpretive sign on a cross-section showing annual rings, Mariposa Grove. *Photo: © Yosemite Conservancy*

and early summer abuts the dense, dark wood produced at the end of the preceding growing season. By measuring the distance across an annual pair of light and dark wood rings, the amount of annual radial growth can be determined.

The quality of the site where a tree grows greatly affects its radial growth rate. A giant sequoia 6 feet (1.8 m) in diameter growing in a favorable site with water available in summer and fall may be only a few hundred years old. Meanwhile, another sequoia, also 6 feet (1.8 m) in diameter, growing atop a dry ridge may be over one thousand years old. When growing in favorable locations with ample water, giant sequoias one hundred years or older can add as much as 1 foot (30 cm) to their diameter every one hundred years.

Several factors can influence the accuracy of tree ring counts. Although each ring usually marks a year of growth, sometimes rings fail to encircle the entire tree. As a result, the number of rings may vary slightly from one radius to another within a given cross section. In addition, it is necessary to estimate how long it took the tree to reach the height on its trunk where the rings are counted. Given these types of variables, ages determined by tree ring counts are only estimates, albeit good ones.

Annual growth rings may be counted either on a recently cut stump or on a core removed from an intact trunk with an instrument known as an increment borer. Increment borers are too short to measure a tree of sequoia proportions, so cut trunks (or extrapolative formulae) are needed.

Giant sequoias are not the oldest known living things, but they are among the most ancient. To date, the bristlecone pines of the arid mountains of the Great Basin are accepted as the oldest. Some of them live to be at least 4,600 years of age, and a few may reach 5,000 years in their lifetimes. The oldest known giant sequoia is thought to be the now-dead Muir Snag in Converse Basin, in Giant Sequoia National Monument. It is estimated to have lived for at least 3,500 years. John Muir counted 4000 rings on a burned snag, but such a source would be difficult to count accurately; this number has never been duplicated by other observers.

Naming the Giant Sequoia

In contrast to the enduring nature of giant sequoias, people have debated its name since its discovery by non-Indian people. The most familiar of its common English names are big tree, Sierra redwood, and giant sequoia. Lesser-known common names include Wellingtonia, mammoth tree, and the distinctive American Indian name *wawona*.

Perhaps more striking is that no less than thirteen scientific names have been applied to this gigantic tree, starting with *Wellingtonia gigantea* in 1853. Soon thereafter, it was renamed *Sequoia gigantea*

Early morning sunlight, Mariposa Grove. *Photo: Jane Rix/Shutterstock.com*

based on the assumption that it could be placed in the same genus as the coast redwood (*Sequoia sempervirens*). Eventually, in 1939, it was given its present binomial: *Sequoiadendron giganteum*, which literally translates to "the giant sequoia tree."

As an interesting sidenote, the genus name *Sequoia* was first applied to the coast redwood in 1847 by Austrian botanist Stephan L. Endlicher. The term has been thought of as a Latinized version of Sequoyah, the name of a remarkable Cherokee man who developed a written version of his people's language. Others contend, legitimately, that the word "sequoia" was derived from the Latin *sequor*, which means "following," referring to the fact that the Sequoia and Sequoiadendron of North America are the evolutionary followers of similar species that are now extinct or, more likely, that the botanist who named the genus recognized their seed counts following in a classification sequence with other conifer groups.

Despite the taxonomic confusion surrounding the giant sequoia, it is clearly in the redwood subfamily of conifers, with the coast redwood being its closest relative. And given that the coast redwood was also for a time called a sequoia (and remains the only living representative of the genus *Sequoia*), the common name "giant sequoia," which is reflected by its scientific name (now modified to *Sequoiadendron*), fits the big tree well and points to its shared evolutionary history with the coast redwood.

Giant Sequoia and Coast Redwood Comparison

Although the coast redwood and giant sequoia are considered to be close relatives, the two species differ in numerous ways. In general, they have these traits in common: being evergreen, bearing cones, having reddish fibrous bark, lacking resin cells, having an abundance of tannin, and developing reddish heartwood (the older, nonliving wood at the center of the tree). The following chart expands on the similarities and differences between these two majestic trees.

CHARACTERISTIC	GIANT SEQUOIA	COAST REDWOOD
Base Diameter	Generally 26–36 feet (7.9–11 m), but up to 69 feet (21 m)	Up to 27 feet (8.2 m)
Height	Up to 312 feet (95 m)	Up to 379 feet (115.5 m)
Age	Oldest known 3,500 years; greatest reported age 4,000 years	Oldest known 2,200 years; greatest reported age 2,200 years
Bark	Rich cinnamon-brown color; deeply furrowed; and as thick as 2.5 feet (0.8 m) at ridges, but generally 1–2 feet (0.3—0.6 m) thick at base of large trees	Dull gray-red, shallowly fissured, 6–12 inches (15–30 cm) thick at the base of large trees
Leaves	Small, stout, and short, 0.4–0.6 inch (1–1.5 cm); pressed close to the stem; evergreen; shed while attached to branchlets	Of two kinds, one resembling those of the giant sequoia, the other flat, needlelike, in two rows; evergreen; shed while attached to branchlets
Roots	Spread to 150 feet (46 m) from the base of the tree; most in the upper 10 feet (3 m) of soil, but there may be roots that go very deep	Spread to 50 feet (15 m) from the base of the tree, in the upper few feet (1 m) of soil
Burls	Few burls, and unable to grow leaves when cut from the tree	Common, and able to grow new leaves when cut from the tree
Cones	2–3 inches (5–7.5 cm) long; usually 34 scales arranged in spirals; mature in second season and may be retained green and growing for more than 20 years	About 1 inch (2.5 cm) long; 14–24 scales arranged in spirals; mature and fall at end of first season
Seeds	In two rows on scales; average 200 per cone	In one row on scales; average 60 per cone
Reproduction	Only by seeds	By seeds, and by root or crown sprouts
Shade Tolerance	Young trees not tolerant of shade	Young trees moderately tolerant of shade
Neighbors	Usually growing among other conifers	Often in nearly pure stands
Chromosomes	22 per body cell	66 per body cell
Horticultural Uses	Extensive use as an ornamental throughout temperate parts of the world	Extensive use as an ornamental throughout warmer parts of the world
Timber Uses	Wood brittle in old trees but equal to coast redwood in young trees; downed trees seldom utilized	Wood notably resistant to decay; much used in construction

The Fossil Record and the Evolution of Redwoods

Giant sequoias are members of the redwood subfamily (Sequoioideae), which lies
in the cypress family (Cupressaceae). For
much of the twentieth century, taxono-
mists recognized seven families of conifers,
with two of these known as Taxodiaceae,
or redwoods, and Cupressaceae. Then,
in the late twentieth century, genetic
research confirmed that Taxodiaceae was
in fact part of Cupressaceae and the sep-
aration of the two families was no longer
viable. The combined family is known as
Cupressaceae.[5] The redwood subfamily
now has just three member species, each
in its own genus: *Sequoia sempervirens* in
California and Oregon, *Sequoiadendron
giganteum* in California, and *Metasequoia
glyptostroboides* in Hubei, China. However, the fossil record is rich with ancient
species from the the three genera which
first made an appearance in North America and eastern Asia in late Jurassic time,
about 150 million years ago.

The number of species in each genus
proliferated, and these species flourished
across much of North America, western
Europe, and eastern Asia from late Cre-
taceous time, about 75 million years ago,
through middle Palogene time, 30 to 40
million years ago. During that time North
America, and the world in general, was
much warmer and wetter, with subtropical
and even tropical conditions and vege-
tation prevailing into the midlatitudes.
Metasequioa and *Sequoia* species thrived
during this warmer and wetter time.

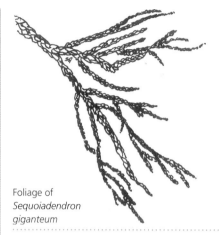
Foliage of
*Sequoiadendron
giganteum*

Foliage of *Sequoia sempervirens*

Foliage of *Metasequoia glyptostroboides*

Beginning in middle Palogene time, the global climate began to change, with the Northern Hemisphere becoming cooler and, in summer, drier. As this trend continued, most species of the subfamily Sequoioideae went extinct, and the rest became less widely distributed and abundant. The three species that remain today have retreated to three isolated points in eastern Asia and western North America. The coast redwood is confined to a region stretching from coastal southern Oregon to central California. The giant sequoia is confined to midelevations of the western Sierra Nevada. The dawn redwood is found only in central China.

Human knowledge of the dawn redwood has a fascinating history. In 1941, Shigeru Miki, a Japanese paleobotanist, formally described the genus *Metasequoia* from the fossil record. He gave the name dawn redwood to a species from Japan and China thought to be long extinct. Then, during wartime in 1943, a chance visit by Chan Wang (Zhan Wang), a Chinese forester, brought the startling news that a tree with very similar characteristics was alive and well in a remote valley in western Hubei Province. Eventually, in 1948, this only surviving species of the genus *Metasequoia* was given the specific name *glyptostroboides*. In 1947 Wan-Chun Cheng (Wan-Jun Zheng), a professor of dendrology at the National Central University, informed E. D. Merrill of the Arnold Arboretum at Harvard University about the discovery. In the winter of 1947 to '48, Merrill received the first seeds from Cheng, an event that was reported widely in newspapers across the United States. Soon thereafter, the famed paleobotanist Ralph Chaney of the University of California, Berkeley, visited the *Metasequoia* discovery site and was also instrumental in protecting the tree and disseminating its seeds. Many communities worldwide are now graced with these pleasing relics of ancient days.[1]

The dawn redwood has several distinct characteristics that distinguish it from the giant sequoia. The most outstanding is that it is deciduous, with its needlelike leaves turning brown and falling from the tree each autumn. In contrast, the giant sequoia retains its green foliage year-round.

The leaves of the dawn redwood look much more like those of the coast redwood than the giant sequoia's scaly foliage. The tiny cones are also more like coast redwood cones than the egg-sized giant sequoia cones. Dawn redwood trunks are noted for the "armpit" hollows under each branch.

Like both the coast redwood and the giant sequoia, the dawn redwood had an extensive range millions of years ago but now has a very limited natural range in China. In its native haunts, the dawn redwood may reach heights of 200 feet (61 m), whereas the giant sequoia is the largest of all trees, exceeding 300 feet (91 m) in height and much greater diameters than seen in dawn redwoods. It does grow well in other places, such that the largest known dawn redwood lives not in China but in New York state.

Distribution of the Giant Sequoia

The entire native range of the giant sequoia is an area only 250 miles (400 km) long by 15 miles (24 km) wide on the western slope of the Sierra Nevada of California. The trees are primarily found at elevations between 4,600 feet (1,400 m) and 7,000 feet (2,130 m). However, the lowest-elevation (naturally occurring) tree grows at 2,700 feet (820 m) and the highest at 8,900 feet (2,710 m). Sixty-five groves are recognized as distinct, but some of the larger groves have been split into more than one by name.

The northernmost stand of giant sequoias, the Placer County Grove, is located within the American River watershed in the Tahoe National Forest and consists of only six large trees growing at an elevation of 5,200 feet (1,580 m). The southernmost is the Deer Creek Grove, located within Giant Sequoia National Monument; it has been logged in part but still has several large giant sequoias.

The northern two-thirds of the range includes only eight groves (including Yosemite's three) and each is relatively small in extent. The remaining fifty-seven groves are in the southern third of the range, and many of them contain thousands of large sequoias. The largest grove is the Redwood Mountain Grove in Kings Canyon National Park and Giant Sequoia National Monument; it covers 3,100 acres (1240 ha) and has several thousand big trees. Altogether, the sixty-five groves cover about 35,600 acres (14,400 ha), of which more than 95 percent are on public lands.

The fact that the giant sequoia occurs in distinct groves, some widely separated, has intrigued people since first it was noted. What could account for this? John Muir was among the first to suggest that the most recent period of glaciation may have divided a once-continuous belt of sequoias. The fossil pollen record taken from meadow sediments indicates that prior to about 4,500 years ago, during a period of hotter and dryer climate, giant sequoias were relatively rare. During this time, giant sequoias were even more restricted to the moistest sites, and groves were smaller than they are today.

The current understanding is that the ancestors of today's giant sequoias were once widespread across the western U.S. During the glacial and interglacial periods of the Pleistocene epoch that ended approximately 12,000 years ago, the extent of this ancestral species waxed and waned. After the last glacial episode ended, the distribution of giant sequoia groves was probably very similar to that of today. Since the relatively hot and dry period mentioned above, the groves have slowly expanded in size and numbers of giant sequoias, although the locations of the groves are believed to have remained remarkably stable.[1, 2, 3]

Giant sequoia groves are confined to locations with high soil moisture—a characteristic that's typically maintained by geomorphic and hydrologic conditions in our Mediterranean climate regime.[4]

Although some of the groves appear to be in a healthy condition and have enough young trees to replace the old ones when they die, many small groves lack adequate numbers of saplings and younger trees to replace the older adults. The factors that contribute to this situation are numerous and complex, but the most important factor is probably the absence of fire. Although fire may kill many giant sequoia seedlings and saplings, it can also kill off many trees of competing species, such as white fir. By removing these competitors and creating canopy gaps that promote new giant sequoia germination, the giant sequoia actually is favored by frequent, low-intensity fires.

Giant Sequoia Ecology and Life History

Ecology, the study of the interdependence of living things and their environments, does much to illuminate the giant sequoia's place in nature. Although giant sequoias appear to be the dominant species within their groves due to their massive size, they are usually only a minor component of the overall forest. Other tree species are more abundant by sheer numbers, such as white fir, Douglas-fir, sugar pine, incense cedar, Jeffrey pine, and ponderosa pine.

The life story of giant sequoias is one of survival in the face of disasters that

A diversity of tree species, Mariposa Grove. *Photo: © Yosemite Conservancy/Ryan Kelly*

destroy lesser trees. This mammoth tree is faced, as are all other living things, with crucial periods in its life history. From struggling seedling to aged giant, the tree is confronted with adverse forces.

The seedling just emerging from the forest floor may die in its first season of life as it lifts its first leaves to the summer sun. Forest insects, including camel crickets and caterpillars, could chew off the leaves or girdle the diminutive stem. Excessive heat may dry and kill the stem, or underground molds may attack the roots. Perhaps the greatest of all natural threats, periodic droughts, can cause the roots and leaves of seedlings to wither and die.

If a seedling survives all of these hazards (and more), it may then start on a living journey that can last more than three thousand years. Up until about four hundred years of age, death rates can be quite high. Some of the threats, drought included, remain the same, but during this time shading from adjacent trees starts to take the greatest toll. Giant sequoias require abundant light. If a young tree grows in an area with little or no direct sunlight, it will be in trouble. However, should it survive to grow above neighboring trees, it will ultimately gain access to abundant sunlight.

As with other conifers, when a giant sequoia matures, its newer, higher branches shade out its lower branches, which die and eventually fall to the forest floor. Therefore, in older age only the top half of the tree bears branches. This, combined with the tree's thick, fire-resistant bark, enables the tree to survive repeated fires.

Fire-resistant sequoia bark, Merced Grove. *Photo: © Dale Ashlock*

The thick bark, which on a mature sequoia is often 1 foot (0.3 m) thick near the base of the tree, and which may reach 2.5 feet (0.8 m) on exceptional specimens, insulates the underlying living tissue from the heat of fires. On sequoias just one hundred years old, the bark is thick enough to allow them to withstand fires that kill adjacent white firs.

However, repeated fires can still burn through the thick bark at the base of a giant sequoia, leading to a fire scar, or cat-face, that exposes the tree's heartwood. Once the bark is removed by fire, this scar could continue to grow in size with each subsequent fire. Eventually, the scar may consume all of the heartwood of the lower tree, leaving just the outer living cambium and bark still intact around most of the base of the trunk. A tree in this condition can survive for decades or even centuries, but it will be more susceptible to toppling during strong winds.

Overall, the giant sequoia has adapted well to fire. In fact, fire is critical to the tree's reproduction, creating a number of conditions that promote germination of seeds and growth of seedlings. These include allowing the seeds fall onto bare mineral soil, sterilizing the soil and thus preventing disease, providing a flush of nutrients from recently burned wood and organic matter, clearing the forest of competing trees, and creating canopy gaps that bring sunlight to the emerging seedlings. Although giant sequoia seeds can germinate among fallen branches and leaves on an unburned forest floor, such seedlings often die because all of the threats they face, described above, are more prevalent in organic debris. In addition, by clearing the forest floor of organic litter, fires make it easier for the roots of

young trees to quickly reach life-sustaining moisture.

Fire also promotes release of seeds by giant sequoias. In order for their cones to open and shed their seeds, they must be completely dry. Fire causes hot air to rise, drying and opening the cones high in the canopy. The resulting shower of seeds then fall on a favorable seedbed prepared by that same fire. Thus, at practically all stages in its life history, the giant sequoia either tolerates or is favored by fire. It does not depend only on fire, however, for regeneration.

The giant sequoias shed seeds throughout the year that, if they fall on exposed soil, may produce new trees. One of the major factors in turning up new soil is the falling of trees. As their roots are pulled from the earth, the pit that remains

Low-intensity fire, Tuolumne Grove. *Photo: Courtesy of NPS*

provides a suitable substrate for seedling sequoias. John Muir once suggested that just the falling of giant sequoias would provide enough suitable soil for young sequoia trees. When large forests are examined for such replacement, however, there are too few seedlings in the pits to replace all the trees that have fallen. So the idea, while intriguing, is unproven.

Release of sequoia seeds without the aid of fire is usually attributable to one of two forest denizens. The first is the Douglas squirrel, also known as the chickaree, which eats the cones of giant sequoias, in addition to those of pines and firs. However, whereas these squirrels eat the actual seeds of pines and firs, they prefer the fleshy cone scales of the giant sequoia cones. Although they do eat a few sequoia seeds, most fall to the ground after the cone is detached from the branch and dries out.

The second is a tiny long-horned beetle, *Phymatodes nitidus*, which attacks the giant sequoia cones in search of food. Although these beetles may destroy a few seeds, they generally tunnel through the central axis of the cone. This prevents water from being transported to the cone, so it dries out, allowing the scales to separate and setting the seeds free. Considering that a mature sequoia may produce fifteen hundred cones per year, with about two hundred seeds per cone, a tremendous number of seeds are available for release via Douglas squirrels and long-horned beetles.

Many other insects interact with the tree in addition to the beetle. More than 140 insect species depend either directly or

Douglas squirrel midden showing a dried cone, scales, and seeds. *Photo: © Yosemite Conservancy/ Pete Devine*

indirectly on the giant sequoia. Some may live their entire lives on one vast branch high in the air. Most are remarkably small and many are well camouflaged, so they escape notice. Small green aphids by the tens of thousands may feed on juices in the foliage. In turn, they are fed upon by the voracious larvae of green lacewings, which fall prey to robber flies. These are consumed by flycatchers, which subsequently are eaten by hawks. Thus, the chain of life is linked from the grand food producer, the giant sequoia, to the ultimate consumer, the carnivorous hawk.

As dramatic as this predator food chain may be, it is pales in comparison to the vast effects of the slow, quiet decomposition of leaves and wood produced by the giant sequoia. Each year, branchlets and their leaves fall to the ground to be consumed by innumerable bacteria and fungi dwelling within the forest floor. And though it may take many centuries, when a giant sequoia falls it, too, will be consumed in the subtle process of decay, the major process of the forest.

Yosemite's Giant Sequoias

Giant Sequoia Protection in Yosemite

ALTHOUGH THEY ARE well north of the main sequoia belt of the Sierra Nevada, the giant sequoias in Yosemite have an outsized significance in not just the history of sequoia stewardship, but in the genesis of the national park concept. In 1857, the Mariposa Grove became only the second sequoia grove to become widely known by European Americans, and it caused a sensation as the rest of the world learned what native Californians had always known: there were more of these tremendous plants in this mountain range. The Merced Grove was mentioned in print in 1858, but then forgotten for more than ten years when the builders of the Coulterville Road stumbled into it and decided to route their toll road through the sequoias. The nearby Tuolumne Grove was also described in 1858.

In the 1860s, increasing private land claims, fencing, and building in Yosemite Valley, and the approach of loggers into the Sierra Nevada's huge forest belt, caused some individuals to worry that these newly revealed wonders could be marred by shortsighted exploitation. The example of how Niagara Falls had been ruined by wildcat tourism development was well known in Yosemite Valley. To

Winter landscape, Mariposa Grove.
Photo: © Ryan Alonzo

the north of Yosemite, Calaveras Grove furnished a comparable problem for those enchanted by the sequoias: There, two trees had been stripped of their bark for display elsewhere, and one tree felled so the stump could become a dance floor and the trunk a bowling alley. Squabbles over ownership and development rights at the Calaveras Grove further tainted the marvels of the forest itself.

Far-sighted Californians feared that the Mariposa Grove and Yosemite Valley could go the way of Calaveras Grove and Niagara Falls, and they sought a new solution for sustaining the glories of the Sierra Nevada for all to see. These concerned citizens included, among others, Galen Clark, Thomas Starr King, Frederick Law Olmsted, Josiah Whitney, Horace Greeley, and Mrs. Jesse Benton Fremont, the wife of explorer and politician General John C. Fremont. Discussions convened by Mrs. Fremont led to an appeal to Washington, DC, in the spring of 1864. Although the capital and the nation's leadership were consumed by Civil War fighting right on their doorstep, Congress quickly passed the Yosemite Grant Act and President Lincoln signed it into law on June 30, 1864.

Never before had any nation's government protected land simply because of its beauty and to make it accessible to everyone for all time. Most historians consider this the beginning of the national park movement, which has since spread around the world as one of our noblest exports and one that benefits all of us today. The much larger Yosemite National Park was established in 1890, surrounding the two original parcels.

Visiting Yosemite's Sequoias

Yosemite National Park contains three giant sequoia groves: the Mariposa, Merced, and Tuolumne Groves. Located in the south end of the park, the Mariposa Grove is the largest and most visited. The Merced Grove, to the north, is the smallest and least visited. All three groves include delightful forest walks to access them; only the Mariposa Grove can be reached by a vehicle (a shuttle bus for most people). All the groves can be visited any day of the year.

As for any outing in the mountains, be sure to study a map to get a sense of the walk you will be undertaking in terms of both distance and elevation changes. Sun protection, drinking water, snacks, and comfortable walking shoes are also important to have with you. If you visit during wintry conditions, be prepared with appropriate clothing and skis or snowshoes.

These sequoia groves are treasures that all of us share. The three groves have also benefitted from recent restoration efforts funded by the public to sustain the long-term health of the trees. The groves can benefit from your helpful attention, too. Whenever you visit, please:

- Dispose of every bit of litter properly.
- Do not carve or write on tree trunks.
- Do not climb on the trees.
- Do not bring pets into the groves.
- Leave cones, etc., where you find them.
- Keep human food away from wildlife.
- Respect other visitors' experiences as they, too, enjoy the groves.

The Three Groves

In 1930, all three of Yosemite's giant sequoia groves—Mariposa, Merced, and Tuolumne—were initially mapped and trees measured by Alfred Bellue.[1] Bellue concentrated his work on the larger trees but also mapped the locations of many smaller trees and areas of recent reproduction. In the 1980s and 1990s, retired forester John Hawksworth mapped and described most of the mature adult trees of the Mariposa Grove. Then, in the early 2000s, National Park Service staff worked diligently to accurately survey and measure all of the large giant sequoias in the Mariposa Grove. In 2013 and 2014, all giant sequoias of all sizes were surveyed in the three groves, providing a thorough picture of grove demographics and the most complete portraits of each tree to date.[2,3]

The two smaller groves—the Merced and Tuolumne Groves—are near the central western border, while the much larger Mariposa Grove is situated near the southern border of the park. Each grove has its own unique attributes, striking individual specimens, and distinctive setting. Indeed, each tree has its own character. Close inspection may reveal a burl, a snag-top, a large fire scar, or an unusual bark pattern.

The groves differ in size, with the Mariposa Grove covering about 550 acres (225 ha) while the Tuolumne Grove covers 24 acres (10 ha) and the Merced Grove encompasses 22 acres (9 ha). In addition to being more extensive, the Mariposa Grove

also stretches across a much greater elevation range. The lower limit of all three groves lies between 5,300 feet (1,620 m) and 5,500 feet (1,680 m) in elevation. The upper limit of the Merced and Tuolumne Groves lie at 5,500 feet (1,680 m) and

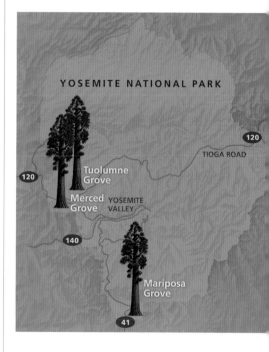

5,800 feet (1,770 m), respectively. In contrast, the Mariposa Grove extends up to just over 6,700 feet (2,040 m), giving it a total elevation range of 1,200 feet (370 m), four to six times the elevation ranges of the other two. Although the Merced and Tuolumne Groves are much smaller than the Mariposa Grove, each still offers visitors a magnificent set of towering trees that are thousands of years old, each with a shared and a unique history.

The Mariposa Grove

The Mariposa Grove was encountered thousands of years ago by people living in the region. While Galen Clark is often given credit for the discovery by a non-native, he never thought he was the first European American there, as there are several accounts of others seeing the trees earlier (see page 5, "Discovery"). Mr. Clark was hunting with Milton Mann in the spring of 1857 when they came across the big trees. He explored the grove thoroughly, made a count of its mature trees, and helped to publicize the grove. It was a sensation.

Development began right away as the Mann brothers built a stock trail up to the grove. Clark built a cabin in the upper area of the grove in 1864, the same season that the grove was protected by the U.S. government. The Washburn brothers built a carriage road from Wawona through the grove. Then they imitated what other entrepreneurs had done in the Tuolumne Grove: they cut a tunnel through a sequoia (in this case a live one), and then they cut another vehicle passage in a second live tree. This road was later realigned and then paved. A campground, ranger station, cafeteria, and hotel were built within the stand of sequoia trees. Private cars drove all through this special forest for decades, their drivers parking wherever they fancied.

Over time, the health and aesthetic of the trees has resumed primacy and this infrastructure has been gradually withdrawn from among the sequoias;

cars were excluded in the early 1970s. In 2014, the National Park Service, with financial support from Yosemite Conservancy donors, initiated a comprehensive management and restoration plan for this grove. Included in the plan and restoration effort were projects that made the grove more accessible for those with disabilities, repaired and rerouted some trails, removed the asphalt road above the Grizzly Giant, and moved much of the parking to an area adjacent to the South Entrance Station.

These actions were implemented to reduce impacts to sequoia roots, restore hydrology that had been diverted, allow for more sequoia habitat, and improve the visitor experience. The changes called for in this expansive restoration effort were designed to reduce human impacts on the grove and its magnificent trees, bringing us to where we are today: a Mariposa Grove where visitors are welcomed and sequoias are sustained for generations to come.

The Mariposa Grove is only 28 road miles (45 km) from Yosemite Valley. Many wondrous sights lie within this grove. Of special interest is the Grizzly Giant, which stands out as one of the largest trees (by total volume) in the grove. The Grizzly Giant summons a sense of mystery, its gnarled and mighty branches protruding in all directions. One of these branches is 6 feet (1.8 m) in diameter—greater than the diameter of the trunks of most other species of trees in its vicinity.

There are hundreds of enormous trees in the Mariposa Grove. The tallest in the grove stands at 303 feet (92 m) tall, and the largest in diameter measures just over 26 feet (7.9 m) in diameter at breast height. There are about fifty trees taller than 250 feet (76 m). In addition to these giants, the grove includes thousands of younger trees, from young adults to juveniles, saplings, and seedlings. These younger trees will one day replace the majestic adults. The total population of sequoias in this grove appears to be healthy, with sufficient numbers of younger trees ready to grow into mature adults. This health is in large part due to the return of frequent fires to the grove.

Starting in about 1870 and continuing until 1971, land managers sought to prevent or extinguish all fires in the grove.

During that time, many shade-tolerant and fire-intolerant trees, such as white fir, were able to flourish in the grove. This resulted in a dense understory of younger and smaller trees, increasing the risk of destructive fires. This buildup of fuels could have resulted in the deaths of many large giant sequoias in the event of a very intense fire. In 1971, the National Park Service deliberately reintroduced fire to this grove after over one hundred years of fire suppression. Between 1971 and 2017 there were twenty-three prescribed fires, and most of the grove has now experienced one to five fires in a short time span. Today, after several decades in which fire has been used as a management tool to restore the ecosystem, the Mariposa Grove has returned to a state similar to what existed prior to fire suppression.

The Bachelor and Three Graces, Mariposa Grove. *Photo: turtix/Shutterstock.com*

The Fallen Monarch and the U.S. Army, 1943. *Photo credit can be found on page 2.*

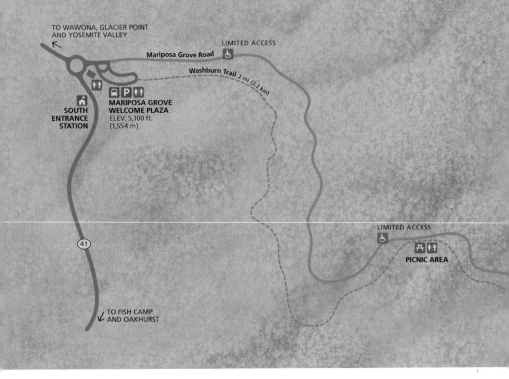

TO WAWONA, GLACIER POINT
AND YOSEMITE VALLEY

LIMITED ACCESS

Mariposa Grove Road

Washburn Trail 2 mi (3.2 km)

SOUTH
ENTRANCE
STATION

MARIPOSA GROVE
WELCOME PLAZA
ELEV. 5,100 ft.
(1,554 m)

41

LIMITED ACCESS

PICNIC AREA

TO FISH CAMP
AND OAKHURST

Visiting the Mariposa Grove

WAWONA POINT
ELEV. 6,800 ft. (2,073 m)

Mariposa Grove Trail
0.5 mi (0.8 km)

Galen Clark Tree

0.73 mi (1.17 km)

0.08 mi (0.13 km)

Perimeter Trail

0.15 mi (0.24 km)

Mariposa Grove Trail
0.3 mi (0.48 km)

0.1 mi (0.16 km)

Mariposa Tree

0.25 mi (0.4 km)

0.45 mi (0.72 km)

0.25 mi (0.48 km)

0.07 mi (0.1 km)

Fallen Wawona Tunnel Tree

0.25 mi (0.4 km)

TO SIERRA NATIONAL FOREST

Columbia Tree

Mariposa Grove Cabin
ELEV. 6,400 ft. (1,951 m)

0.91 mi (1.46 km)

NA

0.15 mi (0.25 km)

0.22 mi (0.36 km)

0.37 mi (0.59 km)

meter Trail

0.45 mi (0.74 km)

0.5 mi (0.8 km)

0.35 mi (0.56 km)

Guardians Loop Trail

0.36 mi (0.58 km)

Perimeter Trail
0.27 mi (0.43 km)

0.2 mi (0.32 km)

Clothespin Tree

Telescope Tree

Faithful Couple

Perimeter Trail

0.94 mi (1.51 km)

0.3 mi (0.48 km)

Mariposa Grove Trail

0.1 mi (0.16 km)

0.75 mi (1.2 km)

KEY

- ‑‑‑‑‑ Accessible Trail ♿
- ‑‑‑‑‑ Secondary Trail
- ‑‑‑‑‑ Horses Allowed 🐎
- 🚌 Shuttle Bus Stop
- 🚻 Restrooms
- Ⓟ Accessible Parking Only
- Ⓟ General and Accessible Parking
- 🌲 Mature Giant Sequoias

Grizzly Giant Loop Trail
0.57 mi (0.92 km)

California Tunnel Tree

0.2 mi (0.32 km)

0.07 mi (0.12 km)

ROAD TO ACCESSIBLE PARKING

Bachelor & Three Graces

0.64 mi (1.03 km)

0.5 mi (0.8 km)

Perimeter Trail

0.57 mi (0.4 km)

0.28 mi (0.46 km)

Grizzly Giant
ELEV. 5,900 ft. (1,798 m)

0.13 mi (0.21 km)

AREA

0 ft.

Big Trees Loop Trail

0.15 mi (0.24 km)

Fallen Monarch

0.25 mi (0.4 km)

TO SIERRA NATIONAL FOREST

Day-use parking is allowed only when shuttle service is not available

N

| 0 | 0.5 km |
| 0 | 0.5 mi |

A TOUR OF THE MARIPOSA GROVE

The Mariposa Grove, located near the south entrance of Yosemite National Park, can be reached by traveling north on Highway 41 from Fresno or by going south on Wawona Road from Yosemite Valley. A shuttle bus transports visitors from the Mariposa Grove Welcome Plaza next to the South Entrance Station to the Grove Arrival Area, a distance of 2 miles (3.2 km). Alternatively, beginning in 2019, visitors may also hike from the main parking lot up to the Grove Arrival Area along the Washburn Trail, also about 2 miles (3.2 km) in length.

When the shuttle is not running, day-use visitors may park in the small parking lot at the Grove Arrival Area. Vehicles with accessibility placards may also park at the Grove Arrival Area and the Grizzly Giant parking area. In winter, the road is closed to vehicles and the grove is best accessed by skis or snowshoes; be sure to be prepared for such conditions.

A short distance before the bus drop-off, the magnificent trees first come into view, their rusty brown bark contrasting starkly with the dull gray of adjacent species. From the bus arrival area you enter into the magnificent giant sequoia forest.

Within the grove, many trails and a variety of passages wind through the grove and informative wayside signs. The map on pages 30–31, which has been derived from the large wayside map, shows the locations of thirteen named trees and other points of interest described below in the order they would be found walking up trail. Begin your tour at the Grove Arrival Area, where the

0.3-mile (0.5-km) accessible Big Trees Loop Trail, with a boardwalk and hardened surfaces, loops past the giant sequoias and the Fallen Monarch.

One note on the measurements given for the trees in this grove: As discussed earlier, standard forestry practice is to measure the diameters of trees at 4.5 feet (1.4 m) above the ground. However, this doesn't work well with giant sequoias because of the irregular, bulging shape of their bases. To help standardize diameter measurements for better comparison, in the Mariposa Grove diameters have been made 10 feet (3 m) above the ground.

The Fallen Monarch

Located along the accessible Big Trees Loop Trail, this tree is remarkable because it remained almost entirely intact when it fell, centuries ago. Old-growth giant sequoias are noted for their brittle wood, so they tend to shatter when they fall, a factor that reduced their value as lumber. In fact, the wood was generally cut into fairly small pieces, and many of the grape stakes in San Joaquin Valley vineyards are from giant sequoias. The Fallen Monarch now measures only a little more than 15 feet (4.6 m) in diameter at 10 feet (3 m) above the ground. The sapwood and bark have long since decayed, but if they were placed back on the tree, the diameter would probably be an impressive 18 feet (5.5 m). Giant sequoia heartwood is slow to decay, and radiocarbon dating has revealed that the remnants of dead trees may endure for up to two thousand years. At various times in the Fallen Monarch's history, stagecoaches were driven on

Roots of the Fallen Monarch, Mariposa Grove.
Photo: © Ryan Alonzo

the trunk and stairs provided access to the upper side (see photo on page 30). Walking alongside this fallen giant and contemplating how long ago it once stood is still a most impressive experience.

Giant sequoias die for a variety of reasons. Some die standing while many large ones topple over. The factors that cause them to fall vary and don't always operate singly. When giant sequoias fall, they usually fall intact, with the system of shallow roots nearest the trunk being pulled up with it, but occasionally the trunk snaps several feet (about 1 m) above the ground. Factors involved in falling are fire scars, decayed roots, carpenter ant galleries, undercutting by streams, extreme heavy loading by snow and ice, strong winds, or a combination of several of the above. If they have fire scars, they usually fall toward the side with the scar. If located adjacent to wet meadows, they typically fall toward the meadow. Most fall in winter or early spring, with storms and wet soil being the final factors in their failure.

On an auspicious note, fewer than five minutes along the trail from the Fallen Monarch toward the Grizzly Giant, on the right before the road crossing, there is great regeneration of sequoias occurring after a 2006 fire. You can see many juvenile giant sequoias here.

The Bachelor and Three Graces

These four trees are an excellent example of giant sequoias' capacity to grow to great size in close proximity (see photo on page 29). Frequently, groups of five to ten trees grow within 50 feet (15 m) of one another. What would ordinarily be competition between individuals is resolved by cooperation. The roots of the trees fuse together and support one another rather than remaining independent. The Three Graces probably are the survivors of a once-dense stand of giant sequoias that seeded here after a fire many centuries ago.

The Three Graces all rise to about 260 feet (79 m) in height, while the Bachelor stands at just under 240 feet (73 m). To see these trees highlighted by the morning sun is one of the many treats the Mariposa Grove offers.

The Grizzly Giant

This rugged tree is located where the Grizzly Giant Loop Trail meets the Mariposa Grove Trail. Only vehicles with accessibility placards may drive directly to a small parking area near the Grizzly Giant. The Giant is the largest or second largest by volume and possibly the oldest tree in the Mariposa Grove. While there are many other individuals that approach this volume, none are believed to be as old. Although it is only a little more than 200 feet (61 m) tall, its massive trunk rises impressively in an almost straight column measuring nearly 31 feet (9.5 m) across at the base. It tapers to about 16 feet (4.9 m) in diameter at a height of 60 feet (18 m) and is still more than 13 feet (4 m) across at 120 feet (36.5 m). The first large limb emerges at a height of 95 feet (29 m) and measures 6 feet (1.8 m) in diameter. Many of the trees near the Grizzly Giant are smaller than this single branch.

The Grizzly Giant has endured many centuries of Sierra Nevada storms, as well as the impacts of human activity. The first roads in the area went right over the roots of the great giant. Well-meaning people constructed all sorts of barriers to keep visitors away from the base of the tree. They dug fence holes that severed the roots, as did holes for the shrubs planted in 1930 to conceal barbed wire strewn around the base of the trunk. Despite these indignities, the noble tree has survived and is growing well. Estimates of the age of the Grizzly Giant have changed over the years; currently it is estimated to be 1,800 years old.[1]

The California Tunnel Tree

This tree is located about 100 yards (90 m) northeast of the Grizzly Giant on the Grizzly Giant Loop Trail. It bears witness to the past propensity of people to cut tunnels through large trees. This one was tunneled in 1895, fourteen years after the famous Wawona Tree suffered the same fate. When winter snows blocked the stagecoach road where the Wawona Tree is located, clever drivers placed the Wawona Tree sign at the California Tree. Thus, for many years it served as a substitute until the road was relocated in 1932. The old road now serves as a footpath, allowing an up-close view of the gradual healing of the great wound.

The California Tunnel Tree is slightly more than 220 feet (67 m) tall and has a diameter of almost 15 feet (4.6 m) at 10 feet (3 m) above the ground. As with the Wawona Tree (described later in this section), burn scars were enlarged to make the tunnel in this tree.

The Grizzly Giant, Mariposa Grove. *Photo:* © *Yosemite Conservancy*

The Faithful Couple

Returning to the Mariposa Grove Trail, the visitor comes to this pair of trees, fused at the base. The name Faithful Couple is a good fit, as these two trees have grown closer together through the years. Even more than the Three Graces, these trees exhibit the ability of giant sequoias to graft to one another. Though many other species of trees can do this, the immense size of giant sequoias makes it a particularly striking sight. The combined trunk is approximately 40 feet (12 m) in diameter near the ground, and the twin columns extend to a height of about 223 feet (68 m).

The Clothespin Tree

A bit farther up the Mariposa Grove Trail is the Clothespin Tree. Repeated fires have consumed so much of the base of this tree that it now resembles an old-fashioned split-wood clothespin. The gaping wound is 70 feet (21 m) high and 16 feet (4.9 m) across at the base, equaling the diameter of the tree at a height of 10 feet (3 m), yet it has not killed the tree, which towers to a height of 266 feet (81 m). Even though most of the original connections between its roots and stem have been severed, the Clothespin Tree appears to be in good health and continues to produce an adequate number of cones.

The Mariposa Tree

Farther along the Mariposa Grove Trail is this tree that was named, as was the grove itself, after the famous gold rush county of Mariposa, within which the grove lies.

The county took its name from a stream that early Spanish explorers had called *Las Mariposas*, meaning "the butterflies." The tree is another fine specimen, standing about 252 feet (76.5 m) tall, with a magnificent 17.5-foot (5.3-m) diameter at 10 feet (3 m) above the ground. Be sure to examine the old fire scar at the base. It provides an excellent example of how new growth of wood and bark can gradually heal fire scars.

The American Legion Tree

There is a granite marker for this tree, which was dedicated in 1921 to the unknown dead of the First World War, but the tree does not appear on the grove map. It is a forest veteran that has survived fire and storm and continues to put out new leaves and cones each year. A tree of fairly remarkable dimensions, it is more than 18 feet (5.5 m) in diameter 10 feet (3 m) above the ground and 248 feet (75.5 m) tall.

The Mariposa Grove Cabin

Along the Guardians Loop Trail sits this reconstructed cabin. Galen Clark, early champion of the giant sequoia, was so impressed with this area of the grove that he built his cabin to host guests at this site in 1864. This cabin was replaced by another in 1885, which was enlarged in 1902. This structure was rebuilt in 1930 and for many years served as a museum for the Mariposa Grove. Take a few minutes to sit on the porch and contemplate what it must have been like more than a hundred years ago when Clark visited this remote mountain haven among these magnificent trees.

A short walk west of the cabin, four giant sequoias stand in a straight line. How did they come to line up like this? Why did this interesting pattern develop? There are at least two possible explanations. In a very wet climate where fires seldom clear the forest floor, a fallen tree in the process of decay may serve as a seedbed. Such trees are called nurse trees because their decomposing trunks sustain young seedlings until the young trees' roots reach the mineral soil beneath. But in a relatively dry climate, such as that of the Sierra Nevada, fire may entirely consume a fallen tree, and thus create a linear seedbed. Therefore these four trees stand at attention all in a row.

These trees range between 213 feet (65 m) and 253 feet (77 m) in height and between 9 feet (2.7 m) and 11.5 feet (3.5 m) in diameter at 10 feet (3 m) above the ground.

The Columbia Tree

Looking west from the cabin, the Columbia Tree is the largest of three visible sequoias. This tree, which has an inverted V-shaped fire scar, is the fifth tallest sequoia in the grove. The Columbia Tree towers to 287 feet (87.5 m) in height and measures about 16.5feet (5 m) in diameter at 10 feet (3 m) above the ground.

In other groves, giant sequoias sometimes reach heights of 310 feet (94 m). This upper limit to growth seems due in large part to problems of water supply to the top branches. Although

50 to 60 inches (127 to 152 cm) of rain fall each year in the giant sequoia belt, it is essentially a rainless place during the late summer and fall. This period of drought stresses the upper branches, slowing their growth. Then, if fires sever root connections, some top branches will die, producing a snag-top tree.

The Telescope Tree

To understand how this tree, located along the Guardians Loop Trail southeast of the cabin, got its name, you have to walk inside it. Then you can see that it has a hollowed-out center, allowing you to look up through it and see the sky above. The processes that produced this phenomenon were probably heart rot followed by fire. Although the heartwood of giant sequoias resists decay fairly well, the older heartwood, which lies nearest the center, becomes less resistant with the passage of time. Once decay has decreased the density of the central heartwood, a fire starting at the base, or possibly at the top due to lightning, may be able to burn out the center of the tree. Repeated fires probably were necessary to create a cavity of the size now evident in the Telescope Tree. About half of the basal perimeter has been destroyed by fire, but in its outer shell the tree retains the three layers vital for the survival of any tree: the bark, the growing cambium, and the sapwood.

The Telescope Tree is only about 200 feet (61 m) tall and 17 feet (5.2 m) in diameter at 10 feet (3 m) above the ground. It probably was well over 230 feet (70 m) tall before it was converted into a hollow cylinder and lost much of its top. Through it all, however, the tree survives.

The Fallen Wawona Tree

This tree is north of the Telescope Tree, farther along the Guardians Loop Trail. While the Wawona Tree was still standing, it was one of the most famous, widely known trees in the world. From 1881, when a tunnel was first cut through its base, until 1969, when it fell, hundreds of thousands of people traveled from all over the world to see the tree a carriage or a car could drive through. Although other sequoias have been tunneled, the Wawona Tree was preeminent. The Scribner brothers cut the tunnel in 1881 for only $75. They selected a live, healthy tree with large burn scars; its diameter was almost 20 feet (6.1 m) at 10 feet (3 m) above ground level, and it was 235 feet (72 m) tall. The tunnel was 26 feet (7.9 m) long, 8 feet (2.4 m) wide and 10 feet (3 m) high.

In the heavy snows of the winter of 1968 to '69, this iconic tree fell—probably in part due to the massive tunnel through its base. It had survived an estimated 2,200 years. Perhaps the fact that it served to bring countless thousands to the Mariposa Grove, where in their pilgrimage they discovered the deeper value of a forest of uncut giant trees, offsets the tragedy of its death.

The Galen Clark Tree

At the far northeastern corner of the grove, near the meeting of the Mariposa Grove Trail and the Guardians Loop Trail, stands the Galen Clark Tree. Although not particularly large for a giant sequoia— only about 16 feet (4.9 m) in diameter at 10 feet (3 m) above the ground and 232 feet (71 m) tall—this tree is unusual on several counts. It is unusually free of fire scars. Its silvery appearance is striking. It is also one of the highest trees in the grove, located at 6,620 feet (2,020 m). And it is probably the first giant tree that Galen Clark saw as he initially entered the grove from the north.

It is fitting that the description of this grove ends with the Galen Clark Tree, because Galen Clark, more than anyone else, first brought people to witness the giant sequoias of the Mariposa Grove. He did a complete count of all the trees in the grove and it's possible that he saw them all as individuals and grew to know them well, almost as friends. He put years of his life into the stewardship of the Mariposa Grove and set a selfless example for all to follow. Just as the bark on the tree named in his honor has an unusual silvery color, each tree in this grove has something unique about it, yet they all stand in quiet dignity, sharing a nobility that transcends even their size—the nobility of true monarchs.

The Tuolumne Grove

In 1868, on his first visit to the region as a transient laborer, a youthful John Muir walked unaware right between Yosemite's two northern sequoia groves, and continued walking miles to the south to see the Mariposa Grove. He ventured into the Tuolumne Grove the following year. Decades later, he wrote up his journals as *My First Summer in the Sierra,* in which he commits far more description to meadow flora than to the majesty of the sequoias. Throughout his life, Muir spent a great deal of time in sequoia forests and worked tirelessly to understand and protect the trees.

The Tuolumne Grove was first noted by European Americans in the spring of 1858. Ten years afterward, State Geologist Josiah Whitney (you've heard of his mountain) referred to it as the Crane Flat Grove, but ultimately it came to be named after its watershed, which is also the name of the county in which it lies.

By the end of the summer of 1870, entrepreneurs from the foothill town of Big Oak Flat brought a toll road through the Tuolumne Grove and up to Crane Flat in order to bring tourists from their settlement to Yosemite Valley. For various reasons, the wagon road didn't reach the Valley floor until July of 1874. In seeking to compete with the rival Coulterville Road, which ran through the nearby Merced Grove (and had reached the Valley floor a month before them), the Big Oak Flat Road management conceived of putting the route right *through* a tree. In 1878 the local Lumsden brothers were hired to cut a passageway for carriages through a standing snag called the Dead Giant, thus creating the first of the several famous sequoia tunnel trees. The forest had been sensational enough, but this tree you could drive a team through was extremely popular.

The Big Oak Flat Road through the grove was eventually made free to the public and was paved. In 1962 the modern highway bypassed the Tuolumne Grove, though cars were still driving through the grove until 1993. That year, the old road was converted to a pedestrian route, and now visitors walk through the Dead Giant.

The Tuolumne Grove includes twenty-four large specimens 6.5 feet (2 m) or more in diameter, as well as dozens of smaller trees. Eleven are greater than 250 feet (76 m) tall. The 1-mile (1.6-km) paved trail leads you down to the grove. There is a short rustic loop trail (0.4 miles or 0.6 km) that leads you among the giant sequoias. A network of split-rail fences along the trail protect the shallow roots from trampling. With thousands of people visiting the grove, each footstep compacts soils that provide nourishment to the trees. Please refrain from walking off the trail.

In addition to the twenty-four larger adults, there are about two hundred young adults, juveniles, and saplings. However, young seedlings are rare. In contrast to the Mariposa Grove, where seedlings and saplings are abundant, there are relatively few very young trees in the Tuolumne Grove. This is primarily because there has been very little recent fire activity in the grove.

Since fire suppression began in the late 1800s, there have been just two fires in the area. One, a prescribed fire in 2005, burned the area east of the old road. Then, in response to the rapidly approaching Rim Fire of 2013, the entire grove was deliberately burned, though at relatively low intensity. The burning undertaken in 2013 has resulted in a large flush of new seedlings and saplings.

A TOUR OF THE TUOLUMNE GROVE

The entrance to the Tuolumne Grove of giant sequoias is located along Tioga Road 0.5 miles (0.8 km) west of the Big Oak Flat Road and Tioga Road junction. Beginning in the small parking lot off Tioga Road, walk downhill 1 mile (1.6 km) on the old paved road to reach the top of the grove. Note that the return hike includes 500 feet (152 m) of elevation gain and is strenuous, and no drinking water is available in the grove. Once in the grove, visitors are strongly encouraged to stay on the old road and developed trails to minimize damage to the fragile shallow roots of the giant sequoias.

The first giant sequoia you'll encounter is located to the left just off the road. With its staggering proportions (15 feet DBH), it looms overhead, greeting visitors to the grove.

Just beyond the first big tree, a paved trail—formerly an old road—splits off

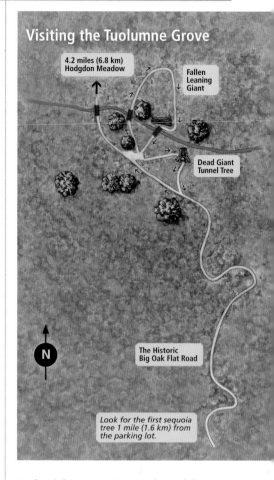

Visiting the Tuolumne Grove

4.2 miles (6.8 km) Hodgdon Meadow

Fallen Leaning Giant

Dead Giant Tunnel Tree

N

The Historic Big Oak Flat Road

Look for the first sequoia tree 1 mile (1.6 km) from the parking lot.

to the right, passes two modest adult sequoias, and then arrives at the Dead Giant, also sometimes called the Tunnel Tree. This once-massive tree was already dead and burned when it had a tunnel cut through its base in 1878 by the Lumsden brothers, through which carriages could drive. If it were alive today, its basal circumference would be about 100 feet (30 m).

Just a little farther down this roadbed lies the picnic area, where the route rejoins the main road. From this location, many large giant sequoias are visible both to the west down the North Crane Creek canyon and to the east. About 170 feet (52 m) west of here stand two sequoias that have grown together to about 6.5 feet (2 m) up at the base, towering 289 feet (88 m) and 291 feet (89 m) respectively. The giant sequoia rarely exceeds this height. Look closely at the tree on the right; it was charred all the way to the crown in the 2013 backburn operation to save the grove during the Rim Fire.

About 250 feet (76 m) beyond the joined trees, near North Crane Creek, lies a tremendous tree that eventually proved too unstable to support its growing crown; in the winter of 2015 to '16, it finally went down. This grand and ancient tree had survived many intense fires that had burned much of its base

Enjoying the Tuolumne Grove. *Photo: © Yosemite Conservancy/Keith Walklet*

and trunk. The fractional base (perhaps 10–15 percent of a full tree trunk) lacked sufficient balance to sustain added weight in the canopy. Back in 1930 its basal circumference (including the now-missing burned portions) was 103 feet (31 m), much bigger than any other living tree in the Tuolumne Grove today. If the original burned base and trunk are included, the tree would have had a diameter at breast height of almost 28 feet (8.5 m). That was once one very big tree.

From the picnic area, a loop trail on the eastern side of the grove travels past two huge fallen trees and several standing adults. Walking next to the fallen trees, you can comprehend the massive size of these giants as they once stood. Some time ago, thoughtless people carved graffiti on these ancient remains.

After returning to the picnic area, consider walking down the old road to enjoy views of large giant sequoias off to the left, down in the North Crane Creek canyon. About 0.2 miles (320 m) from the picnic area stands a cluster of large trees marking the lower end of the grove. From here, you can return to the parking lot by walking up the same route.

The road continues downhill through old-growth coniferous forest about 5 miles (8 km) to emerge at Hodgdon Meadow Campground and the Big Oak Flat Entrance Station on Highway 120. You might consider arranging for someone in your party to drive a shuttle so you can enjoy this quiet descent.

The Merced Grove

In the spring of 1858, a grove of sequoias was mentioned in print as being "discovered" about a mile west of the Coulterville Trail. In 1871 and '72, the crew building a toll road from Coulterville to Yosemite Valley rediscovered the grove and it was decided to route their road through it in the hope that doing so would draw more traffic. The road company owner called it the Merced Grove after the river into which these slopes drained.

The Coulterville Road was the first road to reach the floor of Yosemite Valley, in 1874. For almost twenty years tourists had endured the discomfort of the saddle or travel by foot to witness Yosemite's wonders. Travel by carriage was still slow, dusty, and rough, but it was much more comfortable, and a boon to towns along the way. This road had the virtue of passing a well-known cave (now off-limits) on its way up into the mountains.

A ranger cabin was built in the grove in 1915 to serve as an entrance station along the roadway to Yosemite Valley. In 1924 an incline railway was built from the Merced River to reach the elevation of the big sugar pines. Rail lines intended for hauling timber reached out in several directions from the top of the incline; the flat part of the trail at the start of the walk is one of these old logging railroad beds. Shortly after the walk starts downhill visitors are on the old carriage road that was the first to reach Yosemite Valley.

The Merced Grove, located about 6 road miles (10 km) southwest of the

Old ranger cabin, Merced Grove. *Photo: © Dale Ashlock*

Tuolumne Grove, consists of thirty-one large giant sequoias, with sixteen of these being over 250 feet (76 m) tall. This least visited of the three groves has a special charm due to its relative isolation and intimate setting along Moss Creek. Colorful and delicate wildflowers abound at the bases of the giants, forming a pleasing contrast. The historic Coulterville Road (nominated to the National Register of Historic Places), which now serves as a trail through the grove and beyond, was opened in 1874 and passes directly by several majestic giant sequoias, affording intimate encounters with these magnificent trees. Many others can be seen both downhill and uphill from the road. In all, the experience in this grove is peaceful.

In addition to the thirty-one larger adults, the grove includes about 140 younger adults, juveniles, and saplings. However, young seedlings are rare here, as they are in the Tuolumne Grove, because this grove also lacks an active recent fire history. Since the late 1800s, it has only experienced three prescribed fires, in 1976, 1977, and 1990.

The National Park Service has used prescribed fire frequently to stimulate regeneration within the Mariposa Grove. A similar approach, involving more frequent or more intense prescribed or natural fires, will probably be needed to promote regeneration in the Tuolumne and Merced Groves. Future fires or other active management is necessary to open up the canopy and burn off accumulated duff to encourage seedling success. Gaps in the canopy are crucial for giant sequoia regeneration because they allow light to reach the emerging seedlings and permit more rainfall and snow to reach the ground, nourishing the growing seedlings. Just as important for seedling success is the ability for them to reach the soil, uncluttered by

Mature tree trunks, Merced Grove. *Photo: © Dale Ashlock*

forest debris. Prescribed fire will encourage these conditions.

A TOUR OF THE MERCED GROVE

The Merced Grove is accessed from a small parking lot along Big Oak Flat Road, 4 miles (6 km) east of the Big Oak Flat entrance, located 4 miles (6 km) west of its junction with Tioga Road. From the parking lot, walk south along the old logging railroad bed (now a trail), which runs perfectly flat to begin with. After about 0.75 Miles (1.2 km), turn left and pass through a gate (not shown on map) to continue down the old Coulterville Road (also now a trail) into the grove. Note that the return hike is 1.5 miles (2.4 km), includes 500 feet (152 m) of elevation gain, and is strenuous. No drinking water is available in the grove. Upon entering the grove, please stay on the trail to limit damage to the fragile shallow roots of the trees.

The first giant sequoias are immediately adjacent to the trail: a group of five large specimens lined up like giant columns, greeting visitors to the grove. These trees probably all got their start at about the same time, perhaps following an intense fire that set the stage for emergence of new seedlings.

Continuing down the trail, you'll encounter two more large trees growing adjacent to the trail, and beyond them, 1.5 miles (2.4 km) from the trailhead, the ranger cabin, which was built in 1935, replacing the original cabin located back up the road about 100 yards (91 m). There are several adult giant sequoias, along with a few that are younger, around

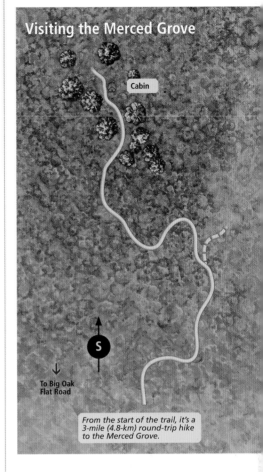

Visiting the Merced Grove

Cabin

S

To Big Oak
Flat Road

From the start of the trail, it's a 3-mile (4.8-km) round-trip hike to the Merced Grove.

the cabin. Continuing downhill, the trail reaches the southern limit of the grove not far beyond the cabin. From here, you can see several massive trees both uphill to the west and downhill to the east, closer to Moss Creek.

The tallest sequoia in the grove is the southernmost one, down toward the creek, towering above the forest at just shy of 300 feet (91.5 m). From the lower end of the grove, you can continue southward to the park boundary if you wish, or turn around and experience the grove from a different perspective on your way back.

Giant Sequoias Outside the Three Groves

Though giant sequoias thrive under particular natural conditions, they have been planted and nurtured in arboreta, botanical gardens, university campuses, and city parks around the world. In addition to Yosemite's three naturally occurring groves, you may encounter other sequoia trees that have been planted throughout the park and its environs.

There are sequoias in parts of Wawona, at Crane Flat, in El Portal, and at Foresta. There are forty-nine sequoias throughout Yosemite Valley in locations that people and trees favored. None were planted before the 1860s, so none are bigger than 5 feet (1.5 m) DBH and all are still in the narrow-spire phase of their life cycles.

The grounds of The Majestic Yosemite Hotel (formerly known as The Ahwahnee) feature the greatest concentration of Valley sequoias. The biggest of these was planted adjacent to the back lawn in 1886, when a dusty stable was established at the site, long before the luxurious hotel was imagined. Rows of sequoias line the parking lot and the former tennis courts.

You can find other sequoias in front and in back of the Indian Museum, in Half Dome Village (formerly Curry Village), at Sentinel Bridge (the site of the old Yosemite Village), and even at Mirror Lake. Perhaps the Valley's most significant are those planted by Guardian Galen Clark around his gravesite. You can find the site in the Yosemite Cemetery, near the visitor center. Mr. Clark was an efficient fellow who excavated his own grave long before he needed it, picked out a flat-faced rock as his headstone, had trail builder John Conway carve his name on the stone, and planted a small garden around his grave, which included the sequoias that he loved. Today those trees are thriving and provide a place where we can be inspired by Mr. Clark's dedication to things larger than himself.

The Future of the Giant Sequoia

While Yosemite's giant sequoias are well cared for within the national park, they are not disconnected from the rest of the world and its challenges. The sequoia/redwood family that used to dominate the Northern Hemisphere's forests millions of years ago has retreated to three small parts of the globe and each remnant pocket is vulnerable. The rapidity of human-induced climate change poses hazards that our sequoias may never have dealt with before. Every day, the National Park Service faces this real and increasing challenge to its mandate to preserve our parks.

All Sierra Nevada forests, including giant sequoias, are vulnerable to a snowline (the generalized belt where

Tremendous cinnamon-colored trunks, Mariposa Grove. *Photo: Steven Castro/Shutterstock.com*

winter rain becomes snow) that is moving upslope. Replacing snowfall with rain means that precipitation runs off instead of remaining on the ground for months and slowly percolating into the soil to nurture big trees, as snow would. Early runoff means early drying of grasses and shrubs, which means that the fire season is suddenly starting earlier than it ever has historically. Denser forests with fuels that have built up during years of fire suppression plus hotter summers add to the severity of wildfire in the Sierra Nevada.

Not only is a longer and more intense fire season more expensive for taxpayers, but it also challenges sequoia survival and reproduction. Some scientists wonder if sequoias are ecologically nimble enough to adjust to these changes, with more of their tiny seeds gradually taking root at slightly higher elevations or on shadier north-facing slopes. Groves may need to be managed more intensively to assure their endurance. Reducing greenhouse gases that we put in the atmosphere and other necessary changes brought about in the fight against climate change will, hopefully, benefit the giant sequoia along with humanity.

A MONUMENT
TO SURVIVAL

THE GIANT SEQUOIA stands supreme among living things as perhaps the largest tree in all of Earth's history. How fortunate we are that our term on Earth overlaps with that of the immense sequoia. Although the giant sequoia only survives in scattered groves throughout the Sierra Nevada, it towers above its neighbors with a quiet majesty born of its millennia of survival while others came and went. It stands with solid grandeur on dry mountain slopes and moist meadow borders, and as Muir notes in *Our National Parks*, it is, "the first to feel the touch of the rosy beams of the morning, the last to bid the sun good-night."

The humble task of an individual tree's existence is living season after season to produce millions of seeds with the aim of merely replacing itself. The giant sequoia persists because the species has patiently evolved with the world's slow changes, but it now faces a rapidly changing climate. The American people decided more than 150 years ago that this remarkable organism deserved to be protected for all time. As this book in which you've invested rests in your hands, our commitment to the sustainability of the sequoia trees depends on our enduring stewardship of the national parks, the national forests, and other protected places. Think big—like a sequoia—and contribute to the success of these extraordinary forests for centuries to come.

"The first to feel the touch of the rosy beams of the morning . . . ," Mariposa Grove.
Photo: © Yosemite Conservancy/Josh Helling

NOTES

Discovery

1 Scott Stine, *A Way Across the Mountain: Joseph Walker's 1833 Trans-Sierran Passage and the Myth of Yosemite's Discovery* (Norman, OK: University of Oklahoma Press, 2015).

Size of the Giant Sequoia

1 Wendell D. Flint, *To Find the Biggest Tree* (Three Rivers, CA: Sequoia Natural History Association, 2002).

2 David Quammen, "Scaling a Forest Giant," in *National Geographic*, December 2012.

The Fossil Record and the Evolution of Redwoods

1 Jinshuang Ma, "The Chronology of the 'Living Fossil' *Metasequoia glyptostroboides* (Taxodiaceae): A Review (1943–2003)," *Harvard Papers in Botany* 8, no. 1 (2003): 9–18.

Distribution of the Giant Sequoia

1 R. Scott Anderson, "Paleohistory of a Giant Sequoia Grove: The Record from Log Meadow, Sequoia National Park," in *Proceedings of the Symposium on Giant Sequoias: Their Place in the Ecosystem and Society*, technical coordinator P. S. Aune (U.S. Department of Agriculture, Forest Service, Pacific Southwest Research Station, 1994), General Technical Report PSW-151, 49–55.

2 R. Scott Anderson and Susan J. Smith, "Paleoclimatic Interpretations of Meadow Sediment and Pollen Stratigraphies from California," *Geology* 22, no. 8 (1994): 723–726.

3 Nathan L. Stephenson, "Ecology and Management of Giant Sequoia Groves," chap. 55 in *Sierra Nevada Ecosystem Project: Final Report to Congress, Vol. II: Assessments and Scientific Basis for Management Options* (Davis: University of California, Centers for Water and Wildland Resources, 1996), 1431–1467.

4 Philip W. Rundel, "Habitat Restriction in Giant Sequoia: The Environmental Control of Grove Boundaries," *American Midland Naturalist* 87, no. 1 (1972): 81–99.

The Three Groves

1 Alfred J. Bellue, "A Technical Report on the *Sequoia gigantea* of Mariposa Grove" (unpublished report, U.S. Department of the Interior, National Park Service, 1930).

2 Bill Kuhn, "Mariposa Grove Giant Sequoias: Status and Trends and Current Physical Stressors" (unpublished report, U.S. Department of the Interior, National Park Service, Yosemite National Park, 2013).

3 Bill Kuhn, "Save Our Sequoias: Final Report to the Yosemite Conservancy" (unpublished report, U.S. Department of the Interior, National Park Service, Yosemite National Park, 2014).

The Mariposa Grove

1 Nathan L. Stephenson, "Estimated Ages of Some Large Giant Sequoias: General Sherman Keeps Getting Younger." *Madroño* 47, no. 1 (2000): 61–67.